Best Online Christian Schools

Find your perfect Christian online option!

Thomas Nixon, M.A.

Degree Press
Fresno, California

Best Online Christian Schools
By Thomas Nixon

Copyright © 2016 by Thomas Nixon

Degree Press
4073 W. Cortland Avenue
Fresno, CA 93722
info@DegreePress.com

Warning: The author has attempted to accurately portray each school. However, the author will gladly post corrections on his blog at BestOnlineHighSchools.com. He will also post the corrections to BestOnlineChristianSchools.com. Should either website cease to exist, he will ensure that the changes are reflected on his personal ThomasNixon.com blog and in future editions of the book.

Both AP and Advanced Placement are registered trademarks of The College Board.

Table of Contents

Chapter 1: Online Christian Schools   1

Chapter 2: Frequently Asked Questions   7

Chapter 3: School Profile – Liberty UOA   15

Chapter 4: Ten Steps to Online Success   19

Chapter 5: School Listings   21

Publisher Information   48

The Author   43

Chapter 1:   Online Christian Schools

This is the first time in history that the teacher, student, and content do not have to be in the same place.

--Willard Daggett, President, International Center for Leadership in Education

Online schools have now become quite common. It is not surprising that, as online schools have grown, the reasons for wanting to use such options has grown as well including:

- Homeschoolers who want to use digital content;

- Students who need an alternative location due to interests in sports or visual/performing arts; or

- Students and families who have concerns about the traditional public school system.

That being said, there are as many reasons for wanting an online education as there are people seeking one. One reason for choosing an online school is to be able to attend a Christian one.

Online schools are becoming the schools of choice for a diverse population of students. For some, they provide a way out of traditional high schools and for others they offer a second chance at earning a diploma. Whatever the reason, online programs can be a convenient and sensible solution for many students. However, it is not necessarily an easy task to determine which are good choices and which are not.

And, should you have any doubt, making the right choice is the difference between a piece of paper that is worth something and one that is not. All things being equal, and in this case they must be, it is much better to choose carefully.

How you go about selecting an online school can depend significantly on what your ultimate goal might be. While there are many possible goals, they tend to break down into two distinct choices:

- You wish to earn a high school diploma to improve your chances at getting a job or entering the military (see Chapter 2). College, at this point, is not something you are actively considering; or

- You wish to attend a college and you either feel the need or it is a stated requirement that you first earn a high school diploma.

Certainly both are valid reasons for considering earning a high school diploma online.

Statements of Faith

Christian schools often have statements of faith, doctrine, or something similar. This lays out in specific detail what the school believes and, in some cases, how it has created its online courses.

So what does this mean? The answer to this question varies widely depending on the school. There are some Christian schools that have these statements and the expectation is that you believe what they believe. Others have these statements, but allow for differences in theological interpretation. Still others, have nothing at all.

Criteria

Whatever the reason, choosing a school requires that you look at a number of criteria. The criteria below should be considered the minimum acceptable standards for selecting an online school:

- The school should be accredited by a regional or national accreditor recognized by the Council on Higher Education Accreditation or by the U.S. Department of Education. Other possible recognition includes that from state departments of education and public school districts.

- For full-time schools, there is a marked preference for schools to have been in operation for at least two years. That being said, what is more important is that the system has experience offering high school courses.

- You should be able to determine through its website or printed materials who owns and/or operates the school. This should include the names of employees.

- It should have professionally-designed marketing and promotional materials. While this may seem simplistic, schools that have printed materials tend to be more established and much less likely to be a poor choice. These materials could be in PDF files.

As has been explained, these are minimum requirements. If you have questions about specific schools, posting a question or two at the Best Online High Schools or the Best Online Christian Schools websites is a good place to start.

The Good Online Candidate

After determining whether it is a good choice in general, you should also determine if it is a good choice for you and whether you are a good choice for online learning.

The first place to start is to determine if you are an independent worker. It takes more dedication to complete an online course than it does to complete a traditional classroom-based course. If you are not able to work independently, you are opening yourself up to a major challenge.

Online courses come in two basic formats: limited time and less-limited time. In other words, some courses are structured within traditional quarters or semesters, while the completion date for others is farther in the future. Neither is better than the other, but understanding your own learning style can help you make better choices with regard to time.

If you find that you work better when you have very specific deadlines, a more traditional schedule likely works best for you. However, if you like things to be more open-ended or there is the possibility that you might need extra time, you should consider that second option. Be careful with that second option, though, because this can be one of the ways that students never finish their courses.

As mentioned before, online courses require real dedication to finish. How can you know if you are able to do this? Take a look at what you have accomplished in your life. Have you ever:

- worked for yourself? The same skills that are required to be your own boss are what are required to be a successful online student.

- completed tasks on a regular basis without being asked? The key component there is "...without being asked."

What are some other possibilities? Climbing a mountain is a good metaphor for what you will need to endure. You get the idea. You can be successful if you have not done these sorts of things, but it certainly makes it all that much harder.

The Role of the Family

If you find yourself lacking in the skills necessary to be a good online candidate, all is not lost. Many of the more successful online learners rely on their families, whether that is parents or spouse, to provide them with the necessary support to be successful. Sometimes all it takes is asking for the extra help.

Chapter 2: Frequently Asked Questions

The future of online learning is clearly one of increased usage by all sectors of education, kindergarten through postgraduate study.

--Michael Lambert, executive director, Distance Education & Training Council

Asking the right questions is your first step on the road to being an online school student. Knowing the right questions to ask can be problematic.

The questions answered below are a beginning, but you will want to ask many more questions of potential online schools. It is a very good idea to get as much information on a variety of schools before making your decision.

Why should I consider an online school?

Online schools can be a good choice for several reasons. If you are an older student, you may not wish to go to a traditional adult school. By earning the diploma online, you have a mask of anonymity that may protect your self-esteem.

Another possibility is that traditional high school may be working out for you or for your child. Perhaps your child goes to a "less than wonderful" school that does not provide enough opportunities for success. Perhaps your child is having social issues with other students that necessitates leaving the school.

Another possibility is the advantage for learning-challenged students. If you or your child requires more processing time, more time to read, or other accommodations, an online school could be a good choice. While time is not unlimited, you certainly have more available than from your local public school.

Why should I choose a Christian online school instead of a secular one?

There is no answer here from me. The reasons for why you would want to choose a Christian school are intensely personal. It could have to do with the curriculum or it could have to do with the teaching location. There are many possible reasons for why you might want to pursue a Christian online school. You need to find your own reason.

Will it help me get into the military?

The answer has recently changed. Online schools used to be classified as Tier 2 for military acceptance. This meant that they were less desirable, but might be acceptable depending on certain factors such as slots available. Tier 2 also includes the GED.

However, all that has changed and online school diplomas were moved to Tier 1 in 2012.

This puts them on the same level as any other high school diploma out there.

Why is it important to choose an accredited high schools?

There are a couple of reasons for selecting an accredited online school. Accreditation ensures you of a minimum level of education. It does not mean that you are guaranteed to get a high-quality education. It will, however, give you an acceptable minimum level.

The other and equally important reason is the acceptability of the diploma itself. A university will accept almost all regionally-accredited high school diplomas, many nationally-accredited ones, and an indeterminate number from unaccredited schools. It is that indetermination that is the problem. The perception is that most unaccredited schools are unaccredited because they do not meet that minimum level. Whether that is true or not is not particularly important. The reality is the perception of those schools.

In a marked change from 2007, it has become clear that recognition by state departments of education and public school districts also have much value. One note, though, is to ensure that the state recognition comes from the department of education and nowhere else. Some states do provide recognition, but it is more of a consumer awareness process and does not attest to the educational quality and often comes from a different department.

Are online schools easier than traditional schools?

It is almost certain that some online schools are easier than some traditional schools. Guess what? California State University, Fresno is easier than Harvard University. Some schools are easier and some are more difficult. This is the nature of education.

Having said that, students typically find online schools more challenging than traditional ones. At traditional schools, you have teachers that will follow up with you and make sure you are turning in assignments. You are also required to be in a certain place at a certain time every day. The same cannot be said about online courses.

Online students need to have more internal motivation. You need to be the sort of person that can get the job done independently. If you are not, that online school experience most assuredly will not be easier than that traditional experience.

How much do online schools cost?

While some online schools are expensive, more than $10,000 per year, others are absolutely free. While cost alone should not determine your choice, it would be foolish to believe that cost is not a determining factor in the selection process.

However, one thing to bear in mind is that the amount of transferable credits from your old high school to your new one can vary widely. While the cost may be more at one school, it might also accept more of your credits. Determining which is the best deal in terms of cost means you need to do your research.

However, if you live in an area that has free online school programs, all bets are off. That is almost always your best choice. Free really is the best price. You should still do your homework, though, because you may discover that you can finish sooner by paying fees to that other school.

However, if you have purchased or borrowed this book, it seems likely that you are looking for a Christian online option. To my knowledge, there are no free options available within that group of schools.

Where are those free online schools located?

Just a few short years ago, there were very few free online schools. With the explosion of charter schools in the 2000s, the number of free online options grew rapidly.

In 2007, a guess was made that the number of such schools would "...continue to grow." There is no doubt that this has come to pass. Many communities now have a local option available. No, they are still not in all states, but certainly in many.

I do not live in an area that has free online schools. Are there less expensive options?

If a free online school is not in your future, it is important to remember that the world is then your oyster. You can go to school anywhere that you choose. While the free schools tie you down geographically, when that is not an option for you, then you can choose a school that is across the country or down the street.

The difference in cost between schools can hinge upon how many of your previous high school credits are accepted at each school. You could find schools that will accept none of those credits and others that will accept all of them.

Are there age requirements?

Some schools do have a maximum age limit, often around the traditional age for high school graduation. Others will accept students up to the age of 21. Still others, have none whatsoever.

Many of the private schools, the commercial programs like Penn Foster High School, allow students of all ages. Other private schools, like Laurel Springs School, are for traditional-aged students.

Where age commonly becomes a factor is in the public programs whether that is a public charter school or an online school attached to a school district.

For many programs, though, there is no age requirement. I have heard often that the reason why someone has chosen to go back and earn a diploma online instead of in a traditional classroom is precisely because they do not want to be with traditional-aged high school students. Nothing wrong with that; if you are thirty-five, you just may not want to take classes with someone who is seventeen (and, likely, they do not want to take classes with you!). That is one of the nice things about online schools; there are many choices and one of those choices is age.

What about all of these high school diplomas through testing programs that I see on the Internet?

Unfortunately, they are scams. The only legitimate way to earn a high school diploma through testing is a program like the California High School Proficiency Exam (CHSPE). Note that this is a program of the State of California's Department of Education. Interestingly, this is a very common question. People often want the easy way out and it seems a reasonable sort of thing. Prove knowledge and get your diploma. CHSPE does this, a couple of other states do as well, and this is also the spirit behind the GED program. However, to be clear, the GED does not provide a high school diploma. It does, however, provide something that some employers will accept in lieu of a high school diploma.

There are no, to my knowledge, private programs that offer legitimate high school diplomas in this manner. Should you run a program of this nature and wish to prove me wrong (and I would be happily proven wrong), I urge you to send me an email at info@degreepress.com.

What courses does a typical online program require to earn a diploma?

While this can vary significantly from school to school, a basic program likely requires between 20-22 units to earn a diploma. The break-down can look like this:

Course	# of credits
Math	3
English	4
Science	2
Social Science	4
Fine Arts	1
Foreign Language	2
Health	1
Electives	3
Physical Education	2

Each credit is the equivalent of a one-year course of study. One thing to bear in mind is that this is one example from one school. Other schools will vary somewhat, but should be somewhat similar particularly with the core course (math, science, etc.) requirements. You may see schools where a year-long course is worth ten credits. Adjust accordingly.

Are there additional requirements beyond the diploma-track if I want to go on to college?

A number of schools have two tracks: a diploma-track and a college-track. While both earn you the diploma, the goals are quite different. It is my recommendation that students take the college-track if it is available. You can always change your mind later about attending college, but it will be much more painful if you need to go back and take courses because your college of choice says you require more.

As far as difference in course requirements, typically you will find that those elective courses above magically become additional courses in science and math.

Will I have a teacher?

The simple answer is that typically you will have a teacher. What exactly that looks like can vary dramatically from school. In particular, the exact level of support given by that teacher can be very little or can be quite significant. This is one of the key questions that you should ask any potential school.

Chapter 3: Liberty University Online Academy

LUOA's primary focus is to deliver a Christ-centered education, built on a biblical worldview that provides an opportunity for a student to grow both spiritually and academically.

--Dr. Jay Spencer, Liberty University

In a recent interview, Dr. Jay Spencer, Academic Dean at Liberty University, discussed why Liberty University Online Academy is a good choice for Christian online students.

Why should a student consider attending Liberty University Online Academy?

JS: Liberty University Online Academy provides a family with the perfect blend of home school flexibility and private school structure, accreditation, and support. LUOA utilizes an independent study format that gives each student a custom experience with his or her learning. The individualized home based education is strengthened by a full staff of licensed certified teachers, academic advisors, and an admissions team to assure each student receives the highest level of academic and administrative support.

LUOA's full accreditation by the Southern Association of Colleges and Schools Council on Accreditation and School improvement guarantees the student is receiving a quality private education.

LUOA's primary focus is to deliver a Christ-centered education, built on a biblical worldview that provides an opportunity for a student to grow both spiritually and academically. In addition to the excellent education a student will receive, every dollar spent for a student enrolled in Liberty University Online Academy is credited toward their undergraduate tuition as a resident campus student at Liberty University! This scholarship opportunity serves as a guaranteed college savings fund at Liberty University and provides a family with a one hundred percent return on their tuition investment.

What are the advantages to attending an online Christian school?

JS: Many families would love the opportunity to give their student a home based education. However, many parents doubt their ability to provide their student with a quality education or simply do not have the time to give their student the attention they need.

Online Christian education allows for a student to receive a home based education without the parent having to be the primary educator or administrator involved. LUOA's unwavering commitment to Christian education assures every family that their student will receive a biblically based, academically challenging educational experience.

What makes Liberty University Online Academy distinctive?

JS: Liberty University Online Academy is built upon a modern, cutting edge technology that is exclusive to LUOA. This platform is built and administered by experienced and licensed teachers with diverse educational backgrounds in their field of study. LUOA's curriculum is written by Liberty University employed faculty and boasts a commitment to biblical worldview and academic prestige.

Describe the relationship between Liberty University and LUOA. Are there any advantages for students who want to go to Liberty University to first attend LUOA?

JS: As a division of Liberty University, the Online Academy benefits from the vast educational resources available in the 7th largest non-profit University in the nation; from technology to curriculum development, the university has provided resources that are unparalleled in K-12 education.

At the forefront of LUOA's relationship with Liberty University is our dollar for dollar tuition scholarship match. Every dollar you spend for a student enrolled in Liberty University Online Academy is credited toward their undergraduate tuition as a resident campus student at Liberty University! Please note that this does not apply to the online program at Liberty University.

In other words, every dollar spent in educating your child at LUOA is like a guaranteed college savings fund at Liberty University.

LUOA graduates who desire to enroll in Liberty University Online rather than attend the resident campus program will receive a *15% discount on regular tuition at Liberty University Online.

LUOA also offers a dual enrollment program specifically designed for high school juniors and seniors who want to earn college credit while still in high school. This program allows students in grades 11 and 12 to begin earning college credit while fulfilling high school course requirements! Every dual enrollment course is taken directly through Liberty University Online giving the student an authentic college educational experience.

Students who meet the required perquisites can even earn their Associate of Arts Degree while completing their high school diploma with Liberty University Online Academy!

Some online Christian schools offer a statement of faith; a description of the Christian principles for the school. Does LUOA have such a document and, if so, what is the importance to families in having one?

JS: LUOA's mission and vision statements can be found at the main "About" page of our website (www.libertyonlineacademy.com). Wit hin our parent agreement page a parent/guardian can find our program goals as well as our expected parental/guardian responsibilities.

At LUOA we believe that it is critical for parents to be in agreement with our mission and goals as an institution. Because this is a home based education it is critical for the messaging between the parents and the student to be synchronous with what they are learning in their coursework. We believe that unity of vision between LUOA and our families is vital to the student's success academically and spiritually.

What role does technology play in the Liberty University Online Academy experience?

JS: Technology plays a huge role in the Liberty University Online Academy experience. All coursework is accessed and completed online. Tests, quizzes, papers, and projects are all completed and/or submitted online. The lab components of our high school science courses are fully virtual offering our students an in depth home based science experience.

A strong internet connection is very important to the student's success. LUOA does not utilize physical textbooks in conjunction with the online experience. All content is in virtual form making technology an essential component to LUOA being an option for a prospective family.

Chapter 4: 10 Steps to Online Success

As with anything, doing your due diligence will make you make successful than just charging blindly ahead. It may sound trite, but do your homework! A good place to start are the ten steps below.

Step 1: Don't go to school online unless you are prepared to work. This is truly one of the best pieces of advice that I can offer. Often people will go back to school, whether that be college or high school, because they think that they are so supposed to do so. While I strongly encourage potential students to consider going back to school, you really need to be up for it.

Step 2: Determine your age. If you are under a certain age (which could be 18, 19, or 21 typically), you might be able to attend a free online school. There are a number of public charter schools that allow for students all the way up to age 21. The catch: It will most certainly be in your state and likely your county (or the one next to it). Free can be a really good price!

Step 3: Do your research on potential schools. Yes, price is important, but that is not the most important issue. There are more expensive choices that are better than some less expensive ones, but the reverse is also true.

Step 4: Narrow your list to three schools. There are hundreds of schools. Before you get too far into your search, begin the narrowing process.

Step 5: Interview the school(s). Yes, you interview them. Find out what kind of support that they provide to students. Find out what a classroom looks like. See if they will give you a sample log-in to look at a course.

Step 6: Decide on a school. Yes, eventually you need to choose one school. Since you will notice that a number of these steps involve school selection, this should give you some idea of how important that selection can be.

Step 7: Ask to speak with a teacher. It is amazing what teachers will tell you that others will not.

Step 8: Set a schedule for working on your courses. Yes, online courses are marketed as you being able to work on them whenever you would like, but that is only partially true. You still must get it all done. Determine how many hours a week you should devote to the courses and then do it.

Step 9: Do your homework. I know that this sounds simplistic, but if I had a dime for every online student who told me they fell behind in their assignments because no one was keeping track of it for them, I would be a rather wealthy person.

Step 10: Keep at it. Don't give up. Remember that the hard work is worth the end results. This is exactly what it says. You will need to put time and effort into this or you will fail. Again. That being said, you can do this. Push yourself.

Chapter 5: School Listings

Below you will see a number of Christian online schools. There are certainly others that exist in the world. Should you wish to get your school listed and it has recognized accreditation, you can send that information to the email address below. Likewise, if your school is listed, but the information is inaccurate or incomplete, send that information to the email address below as well.

info@degreepress.com

SCHOOLS

Alberta Distance Learning Centre
4601 - 63 Avenue
(Box 4000)
Barrhead, Alberta T7N 1P4
Canada
Tel: 780.674.5333
Web: www.adlc.ca
Email: information@adlc.ca
Recognition/Accreditation: Provincial Governments
Grade: K-12
Type: Christian, Free, Public
Diploma: Yes
Cost: Free
If free, where?: Alberta, Northwest

Territories, Nunavit provinces
Teen and/or Adult: Teens
Additional information: Alberta Distance Learning Centre offers several programs including a Christian-based one and a French Immersion one. Students may also avail themselves of Work Experience. Program is available to students living in Alberta and to those traveling with their families. Program was founded in 1923. It has grown to include an online learning program as well.

Alpha Omega Academy
300 N. McKemy Avenue
Chandler, Arizona 85226
United States
Tel: 602.438.2717
Web: www.aoacademy.com
Email: online@aop.com
Recognition/Accreditation: NCA
Grade: K-12
Type: Christian, Private
Diploma: Yes
Teen and/or Adult: Teens
Additional information: Alpha Omega Academy offers over 160 courses. AOA offers the possibility of dual credit (high school and college) for students. Students enroll in a partner college and the school awards .5 credits for each college course completed.

Regina Coeli Online Academy
6429 S. Woodland Hills Drive

Tucson, Arizona 85747
United States
Tel: 520.751.1942
Web: www.reginacoeli.org
Email: admin@reginacoeli.org
Grade: 9-12
Type: Christian, Private
Diploma: Yes
Cost: $3,200 - $3,500 full-time
Teen and/or Adult: Teens
Additional information: Regina Coeli Online Academy is a solidly Catholic online school. It requires significant interaction with teachers. Most classes meet twice a week using interactive live video and text conferencing. Most of its instructors are also currently homeschooling or have homeschooled their own children, so have the requisite experience.

Oaks Christian Online School
31749 La Tienda Drive
Westlake Village, CA 91362
United States
Tel: 855.462.6257
Web: online.oakschristian.org
Email: online@oakschristian.org
Recognition/Accreditation: WASC
Grade: 9-12
Type: Christian, Private
Diploma: Yes
Cost: $7,250
Teen and/or Adult: Teens

Additional information: Oaks Christian Online School is an out-growth of the face-to-face Oaks Christian School which started in 2000. This school offers a college-prep curriculum that includes honors, Advanced Placement, and dual credit courses.

Calvary Online School

1675 Seven Oakes
Road
Escondido, California 92026
United States
Tel: 760.410.8283
Web: calvaryonlineschool.com
Email: info@calvaryonlineschool.com
Recognition/Accreditation: WASC
Grade: 7-12
Type: Christian, Private
Diploma: Yes
Cost: $4200 annual tuition
Teen and/or Adult: Teens
Additional information: Touts itself as the "first tablet only school." It operates in affiliation with Calvary Chapel of Escondido (now called Cross Connection Escondido). Calvary Online School uses the same statement of faith as the church. It does, though, have students from all denominations.

Capistrano Valley Christian Schools Online

32032 Del Obispo Street
San Juan Capistrano, California 92675

United States
Tel: 949.493.5683
Web: www.cvcs.org/academics/online-school
Email: info@cvcs.org
Recognition/Accreditation: WASC
Grade: 6-12
Type: Christian, Private
Diploma: Yes
Cost: $1585 per course
Teen and/or Adult: Teens
Additional information: Capistrano Valley Christian Schools Online is part of the larger Capistrano Valley Christian Schools and has a significant number of students studying off-line. The online school is meant to provide increased flexibility to students. More than a hundred courses are available for grades 6-12 including courses in the Bible. The school asserts that its curriculum exceeds both the national and California state standards.

Ontario Christian School Online
931 W. Philadelphia Street
Ontario, California 91762
United States
Tel: 909.983.4644
Web: www.ontariochristianonline.org
Email: online@ocschools.org
Recognition/Accreditation: WASC
Grade: K-8
Type: Christian, Private
Diploma: Yes
Teen and/or Adult: Teens

Additional information: Ontario Christian School Online offers courses for students in grades 3-8. This includes instruction in the core courses (including Bible) as well as a variety of electives. The school offers asynchronous courses (meaning that there are no set times when your child needs to be online). The online courses, in addition to text, also use video and interactive learning tools. While the school has a Biblical worldview, it is open to students from all denominations.

Orange Lutheran High School Online

2222 North Santiago Boulevard
Orange, California 92867
United States
Tel: 714.998.5151
Web: www.lhsoc.org/olo
Email: young@lhsoc.org
Recognition/Accreditation: WASC, NCAA
Grade: 9-12
Type: Christian, Private
Diploma: Yes
Cost: $9,990 per semester
Teen and/or Adult: Teens
Additional information: Orange Lutheran Online is part of Lutheran High School of Orange County. The courses are designed by LHSOC instructors and, in addition to core courses, also offers communication, business law, accounting, and theology. It also offers Advanced Placement courses as well. Its online

courses are acceptable to NCAA.

Southlands Online School

1920 S. Brea Canyon Cutoff Road
Walnut, California 91789
United States
Tel: 909.598.9733
Web: southlandsonlineschool.com
Email: onlineinfo@southlandscs.com
Recognition/Accreditation: WASC
Grade: 9-12
Type: Christian, Private
Diploma: Yes
Cost: $4900
Teen and/or Adult: Teens
Additional information: Southlands offers a variety of instructional tools including digital textbooks, live teaching sessions, and forums. The website has a video that showcases its online program. The school does have a statement of faith, so you may wish to see what that entails. The school, rightly, points out where its graduates have been accepted for college.

Western Christian Academy

P.O. Box 306
Prather, California 93651
United States
Tel: 800.868.5839
Web: westernchristianacademy.com
Email: westernchristianonline@gmail.com
Recognition/Accreditation: NCA

Grade: 3-12
Type: Christian, Private
Diploma: Yes
Cost: $1462 - $1630 per year
Teen and/or Adult: Teens
Additional information: Western Christian Academy focuses on creating an individualized course of study for each student. Offers annual, semester, quarterly, or monthly payment options.

Additional information: Western Christian Academy has a monthly payment option. The schools uses the "Switched on Online" curriculum. The school does have a statement of faith, so you may wish to see what that entails. WCA offers a "Teacher On Call" feature for families who would like to have access to teacher. Should you not wish to use that option, the cost for the school is significantly less.

Christian Educators Academy
601 Shorewood Drive, G303
Cape Canaveral, Florida 32920
United States
Tel: 321.501.0300
Web: www.highschool-online.com
Email: info@christian-educators.com
Recognition/Accreditation: NWAC
Grade: 3-12
Type: Christian, Private
Diploma: Yes

Cost: $1600 (for 365 days)
Teen and/or Adult: Both
Additional information: Christian Educators Academy offers three different diploma programs: College Preparatory, Standard Academic, and Career Prep. The College Preparatory program is for students who are looking to excel and has a 3.5 GPA minimum requirement. The Standard Academic Diploma is for students who are considering college or career. Students must maintain a 3.0 GPA. The Career Prep Diploma is for students who wish to start work after graduation.

Alpha Omega Academy
804 N. 2nd Avenue East
Rock Rapids, Iowa 51246
United States
Tel: 712.472.6610
Web: aoacademy.com
Email: On website
Recognition/Accreditation: AdvanceED
Grade: K-12
Type: Christian, Private
Diploma: Yes
Cost: $396 full year, per course
Teen and/or Adult: Teens & Adults
Additional information: Alpha Omega Academy is a Christian online school that offers over a hundred courses. AOA offers courses in several formats: Switched-On Online (grades 3-12; online), Switched-On Schoolhouse (grades

3-12; computer-based, but not online), and LIFEPAC (grades K-12; print-based).

Griggs High School Online
12501 Old Columbia Pike
Silver Spring, Maryland 20904
United States
Tel: 301.680.6579
Web: www.griggs.edu/highschoolonline.html
Email: admissions@griggs.edu
Recognition/Accreditation: SACS, DETC
Grade: K-12
Type: Christian, Private
Diploma: Yes
Cost: By the course
Teen and/or Adult: Teens
Additional information: Griggs High School Online is affiliated with the Seventh-Day Adventist denomination schools system.

Livingston Christian Schools
550 East Hamburg Street
Pinckney, Michigan 48169
United States
Tel: 734.878.9818
Web: online.livingstonchristianschools.org
Email: lcsonline@livingstonchristianschools.org
Recognition/Accreditation: NCA
Grade: 3-12
Type: Christian, Private
Diploma: Yes
Cost: $300-475 per course
Teen and/or Adult: Teens

Additional information: The school offers both seat-based and online versions of its Christian curriculum. The school has a doctrine statement that may be of interest to potential students. It offers courses in all the core subject areas as well as electives.

NorthStar Academy
3790 Goodman RD E
Southaven, Mississippi 38672
United States
Tel: 888.464.6280 / 662.892.4380
Web: www.northstar-academy.org
Email: info@northstar-academy.org
Recognition/Accreditation: SACS
Grade: 5-12
Type: Christian, Private
Diploma: Yes
Cost: $345 per semester course w/ teacher
Teen and/or Adult: Teens and Adults
Additional information: NorthStar academy offers an online Christian either led by a teacher or led by parents. It also offers dual credit courses through either LeTourneau University or through Moody Bible Institute.

Eagle Christian School
2526 Sunset Lane
Missoula, Montana 59804
United States
Tel: 406.544.3738
Web: www.eaglechristian.org
Email: eagle@eaglechristian.org

Recognition/Accreditation: NWAC
Grade: K-12
Type: Christian, Private
Diploma: Yes
Cost: $2,600 per year.
Teen and/or Adult: Teens
Additional information: The Eagle Christian School's website provides an online demonstration of its curriculum. The school is also accredited by the state of Montana

Sevenstar Academy
3630 Park 42 Drive, Suite 170F
Cincinnati, Ohio 45241
United States
Tel: 513.612.1029 or 877.877.7040
Web: www.sevenstaracademy.org
Email: info@sevenstaracademy.org
Recognition/Accreditation: NCA
Grade: 6-12
Type: Christian, Private
Diploma: Yes
Cost: $3011 per year
Teen and/or Adult: Teens
Additional information: Sevenstar offers more than seventy online courses for both Christian schools and for home education. It also offers over one hundred thirty dual credit courses from a number of Christian colleges and universities around the country.

Saskatoon Catholic Cyber School
2701 Porter Street

Saskatoon, Saskatchewan S7J 3K7
Canada
Tel: 306.659.7700
Web: www.scs.sk.ca/cyber/
Email: cyber@scs.sk.ca
Recognition/Accreditation: Greater
Saskatoon Catholic Schools
Grade: 9-12
Type: Christian, Private
Diploma: Yes
Teen and/or Adult: Teens
Additional   information: Saskatoon
Catholic Cyber School is part of Greater
Saskatoon Catholic Schools, Saskatchewan's
largest Catholic school division. All courses are
based   on   the   Saskatchewan   Learning
Curriculum   and   students   will   receive
Saskatchewan credit for having completed
these   online   courses.

Lighthouse Christian Academy
610 W. Due West Avenue
Madison, Tennessee 33775
United States
Tel: 866.746.6534
Web: www.lcaed.com
Email: LCAed@aceministries.com
Recognition/Accreditation: MSA-CESS
Grade: K-12
Type: Christian, Private
Diploma: Yes
Cost: $850 (K-8), $950 (9-11), $1,000 (12)
Teen and/or Adult: Teens

Additional information: Lighthouse Christian Academy is a provider of mastery-based Christian education and offers instruction primarily for homeschooling students. The school offers four distinct courses of study: honors, college preparatory, general, and vocational.

Liahona Preparatory Academy
2464 West 450 South
Pleasant Grove, Utah 84062
United States
Tel: 801.785.7850
Fax: 801.785.4723
Web: liahonaeducation.com
Email: melody@LiahonaEd.com
Recognition/Accreditation: NWAC
Grade: K-12
Type: Christian, Private
Diploma: Yes
Cost: $4860 per year
Teen and/or Adult: Teens
Additional information: The Liahona Preparatory Academy is the largest LDS-based Junior High and High School distance program.

Liberty University Online Academy
1971 University Boulevard
Lynchburg, Virginia 24502
United States
Tel: 866.418.8741
Web: luonlineacademy.com

Email: LUOAinfo@liberty.edu
Recognition/Accreditation: SACS
Grade: 3-12
Type: Christian, Private
Diploma: Yes
Cost: $2,500 per year
Teen and/or Adult: Teens
Additional information: Liberty University Online Academy is an online Christian school that serves grades 3 - 12. Students in grades 11 - 12 can dually enroll through Liberty University Online. A unique advantage for students who may wish to go on to be undergraduates at Liberty University is that the university will credit, dollar for dollar, everything that you spend on LUOA toward tuition.

Scholars Online
PO Box 6039
Bellevue, Washington 98008
United States
Web: www.scholarsonline.org
Email: admin@scholarsonline.org
Recognition/Accreditation: NWAC
Grade: 9-12
Type: Christian, Private
Diploma: Yes
Cost: Varies based on Teacher/Course
Teen and/or Adult: Both
Additional information: Scholars Online offers a Christian-based classical education for college-bound students that is challenging.

Coming soon from Degree Press

Free College Degrees (2016)

Test Out of College (2016)

Cheap College Degrees (2017)

www.ingramcontent.com/pod-product-compliance
Lightning Source LLC
Chambersburg PA
CBHW060542030426
42337CB00021B/4394